Early Photographs of Radnor

Early Photographs of Radnor

Photographs by William McKaig
Text by Laurence Smith

Logaston Press

LOGASTON PRESS
Little Logaston Woonton Almeley
Herefordshire HR3 6QH

First published by Logaston Press 2004
Copyright © Laurence Smith 2004

ISBN 1 904396 18 6

Set in New Baskerville by Logaston Press
and printed in Great Britain by
Cromwell Press, Trowbrdge

Location

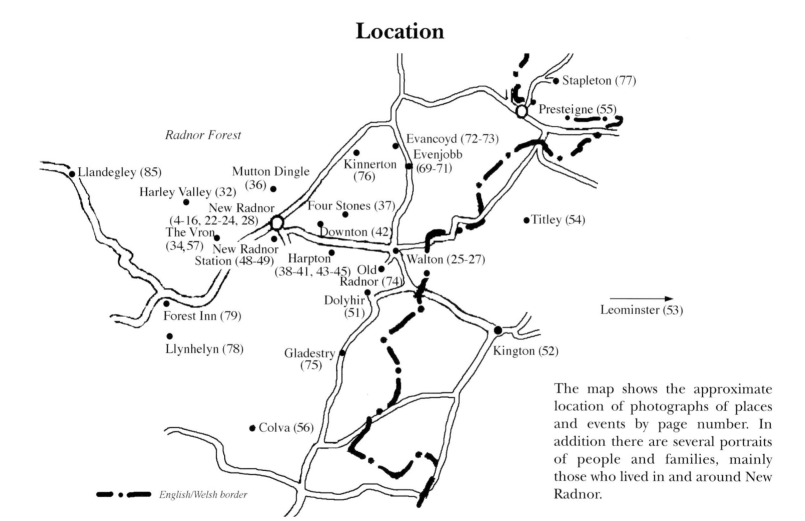

Radnor Forest

Llandegley (85)

Harley Valley (32)

Mutton Dingle (36)

Kinnerton (76)

Evancoyd (72-73)

Evenjobb (69-71)

Stapleton (77)

Presteigne (55)

New Radnor (4-16, 22-24, 28)

Four Stones (37)

The Vron (34,57)

New Radnor Station (48-49)

Downton (42)

Titley (54)

Harpton (38-41, 43-45)

Old Radnor (74)

Walton (25-27)

Leominster (53)

Dolyhir (51)

Forest Inn (79)

Llynhelyn (78)

Gladestry (75)

Kington (52)

Colva (56)

— ·· — ·· English/Welsh border

The map shows the approximate location of photographs of places and events by page number. In addition there are several portraits of people and families, mainly those who lived in and around New Radnor.

Introduction

William McKaig probably picked up his interest in photography from his father, Leonard, who used his camera, at least in part, to produce postcards for local sale. Leonard's main job, however, was to run the school in New Radnor in conjunction with his wife, Susannah, from 1886 to 1910. Before his appointment the couple had lived in London where William was born in 1885, their third son.

Billy, as he was known, left New Radnor's school in about 1900 and set up a cycle repair workshop to cater for the fast growing numbers of tourists who liked to cycle out to the country from places like Birmingham. It is difficult today to imagine the miles of leafy lanes without a single motor vehicle. Learning from his father, he soon saw the opportunity to supply these visitors with mementoes of their trips by producing postcards of the beauty spots of Radnorshire and of the quiet leafy lanes that the cyclists used.

At that time of horsepower and hobnails, oil lamps and well-water, servants and steam trains, The McKaigs were probably the only ones with a camera for miles around. So Billy was called on to take photos of local events and family gatherings, prize bulls, and pets. As a result his photos give us a wonderful glimpse of life in that era, but he also had an artistic eye and his photos benefit from being well composed.

The time it took to set up a half-plate camera on its tripod and the long exposures needed for a picture mean that subjects can look rather posed because people had to keep still for several seconds. But Billy took risks and there are some delightful pictures with a snapshot quality to them. Look at the spectators at the Radnor Valley Agricultural Association Meetings for example. I was amused to read in the School Log-book that the children you see in those pictures should have been at school—their absence on that day was noted and recorded by Billy's father!

The logbook also records an Object Lesson, which until 1900 had been simply a question of copying off the blackboard, but this day the Master decided to take his class on a walk to a willow tree to gather actual specimens of leaves and twigs. This gave more life and interest to the lesson. Billy took a photo of children on just such a nature walk.

The quality of his photographs led to a close friendship with Alfred Watkins, Hereford's polymath of the period, which led to his appointment as Watkins' works manager. This involved a move to Hereford and after 1918 Billy left his photographic business in New Radnor to his unmarried sisters, Agnes and Gertrude. As works manager Billy was required to produce the Bee Meter, a pocket watch-sized light-meter that Watkins had invented. This was the first device to remove much of the guesswork of the exposure time for photographers and had been much praised by Herbert Ponting who had taken stunning photos of the Antarctic for Captain Scott's Expedition.

Soon after, Watkins started to formulate his ideas about Ley-lines, those mysterious straight lines that appear to link some prehistoric sites and notable features in the landscape, and he took McKaig with him on many expeditions to survey the countryside. When he came to write *Early British Trackways* and the still popular *The Old Straight Track* he asked Billy to draw the maps and diagrams. In the records of The Straight Track Postal Club held in Hereford Library, Billy is praised for organizing successful meetings and in his skills with the magic lantern were so much appreciated he was made Honorary Lanternist for the Woolhope Club. In 1931 he married Alice Reeves.

Watkins died in 1935 and in his will left all his photographic equipment to William McKaig, including his three and a half thousand glass negatives. Though twenty years his younger, McKaig died only a few weeks after Watkins, aged 52. The collection of Watkins' photographs eventually passed to Hereford Library and his equipment to the Museum, but the works of Billy McKaig were lost and forgotten.

In 1980 I tried my hand at computer restoration of photographs and several people brought me photographic postcards of New Radnor to enhance. Many of these were badly damaged, being folded, scratched, chipped and torn. They had finger marks and the grime of eighty years on them. But by the magic of computer technology I was able to restore them to their original state.

The postcards had the maker's name or initials on them, for even in those days it had been important to copyright photographs as some card producers were making copies of others' work. I did in fact find one of McKaig's that had been copied in this way.

I was most impressed by the quality of those cards recorded as being by W.H. McKaig and so I started some detective work. When I contacted postcard collectors in the area, they helped me to build up a knowledge of the range of his interests. They also kindly allowed me to make copies of their cards so that I could create an archive of his work. I also asked local families if I could look through their photo albums, and was delighted that many of them contained a postcard or two by McKaig. Other cards came to light after I had shown slides and set up exhibitions of his photos in New Radnor. The most recent addition was brought to me by a visitor to New Radnor, who came to find where his grandfather had been born. The card, which showed this relative standing by a plough, had been sent out to Australia in 1908. Without the generosity of all these people, to whom I am extremely grateful, this collection would not have been possible, and I hope more photos will come to light as a result.

I am pleased to say that 30 glass negatives have also survived in a private collection.

Laurence Smith

Producing a Postcard

At a time of instant images and digital cameras it is difficult to appreciate all the skills that were required in taking black and white pictures in the old way, and how much time and effort it involved. There were no automatic mechanisms and no computer assistance. Every part of the procedure needed the photographer's expertise and judgement.

Box cameras were available in the early 1900s but were really only suitable for summer holiday snaps. 'The possession of a the "cutest camera" and the desire to snap everything will not alter the stern fact that only a minor proportion of desirable objects are well lighted enough to be snapped with success', says Alfred Watkins rather dismissively in his *Manual of Photography*! This was a book that would have been familiar to McKaig.

We know from the size of the glass negatives, $6\frac{1}{2}$ins. x $4\frac{3}{4}$ins., that McKaig used what was called a half plate camera. This camera was made of varnished mahogany and had brass fittings, a separate lens and a leather bellows to allow it to fold up. It was a very attractive looking object but large and heavy and required a substantial tripod to keep it steady. Instead of rolls of film it required plates of glass that had been coated with a light sensitive material.

It therefore took time to prepare and take a photograph. McKaig would have gone into a dark room to find his box of ready prepared plates. He then would have inserted two into a wooden holder called a dark slide, one on each side. Once the camera was set up on its tripod and the lens slotted into its place at the front, McKaig would have opened the shutter so that light from the subject could be focused on a piece of frosted glass at the back of the camera. The lens was then moved forward or backwards by means of a small brass wheel, but in order to see the image and focus it sharply, it was necessary to shade the image by getting under a large black cloth. The projected image was inverted by the lens and so McKaig would have had to become used to composing pictures that were always upside down. When satisfied that the subject was as sharp as he could get it, he would have folded the frosted glass out of the way and replaced it with one of the dark slides, inserting this into a tight fitting slot. He would then close the shutter.

It was then necessary to make some judgements as to the subject and how well it was lit. This next stage involved making a number of calculations that depended on the sensitivity of the plate, how much light was to be allowed through the lens and the actual strength of that light. To help him in this, McKaig would have taken out his exposure meter to obtain an accurate reading of the light. This amazing little gadget had been invented by Alfred Watkins and was called a Bee Meter. Shaped like a pocket watch, it contained a small piece of special paper that changed colour in the light. The time it took to change was all-important, and this time, together with the plate speed and the aperture at the lens were noted. These details were then aligned on special dial that could, with a twist of a thumb, give the correct exposure reading. Exposure times varied from several seconds or a fraction of a second depending on the brightness.

McKaig would then be ready to take a photo, except that he must not forget to now draw back the pate cover! If the subject included people he would have reminded them to keep very still and then he would have squeezed a small rubber bulb to trigger the shutter by gentle air pressure—click!

McKaig would have taken the exposed plates back to his dark room, and in the glimmer of a red lamp, set about the process of developing his own negatives. When they were fixed and washed and dried he could then go on to print postcards. The postcards were made of photographic paper and so they too needed to be developed, washed, fixed, washed again and dried before they were ready.

Alfred Watkins published a useful *Manual of Photography* for beginners, and when you find that he devoted about 35 pages just to the subject of Exposure, you start to realise that the permutations of light quality and shutter speeds and film sensitivity were far from straight forward. But then the other half of his book was given over to the equally testing art of Developing the Negative which involved complicated chemical processes involving quite precise temperatures and timing. Taking a photo in those days required the skills of both an artist and a scientist, and McKaig was certainly an accomplished photographer.

Billy McKaig is seen here driving a friend's motorcycle and sidecar. His passengers, Agnes and Gertrude took over his Photography business when he moved to Hereford. They produced a few postcards but did not have Billy's eye for a good picture

Billy ran a cycle repair shop at the top right-hand side of Broad Street in New Radnor.
His sisters Agnes and Gertrude joined the cycling craze that swept the country at the turn of the twentieth century

Billy, on the left of the picture, is pondering where to set up his next sighting pole to help Alfred Watkins, who is standing in front of the gate, plot another Ley-line. This photo is reproduced by kind permission of Hereford Library and Information Services, which has all the notebooks that record the outings of The Straight Track Postal Club

This is a detail from a view of New Radnor he took about 1910. The low wall running in front of the houses follows the line of the old town wall. The Castle Hill is flanked by trees.

This view from Castle Hill is looking down onto the roof of the Town Hall in the foreground. Opposite are The Eagle Hotel and The Stores with its window blinds out. The School is just showing through the trees and in the distance is the Railway Station. The Smatcher, top right, was then largely a fern covered hill

Originally the 77ft. high monument to Sir George Cornewall Lewis, local MP and Chancellor of the Exchequer who died in 1863, was planned for the top of Castle Hill. The architect was John Gibbs who also designed the monument to Shakespeare at Stratford-on-Avon. The ivy covered Monument House is where the McKaigs lived initially

Children play in a traffic free Broad Street. The house facing at the top belonged to Thomas Gittoes, the blacksmith.

The Minerva Motorbike on the left belonged to Mr. King of Hereford. Myrtle Cottage, with Mrs. Lingen at the door, is now the site of the Radnor Arms restaurant. Dr. Harding, seated at the wheel of the car, owned the first car in New Radnor. PC Rogers can just be seen behind the top hat of Mr. Shewell, and the barn-like building behind him was Billy's workshop. The circular sign on The Eagle Hotel is advertising The Cyclists' Touring Club

Two boys show a keen interest in Dr. Harding's car as it makes its way along a snow covered High Street. There were about a dozen shops in New Radnor in 1906, including a shoe shop and cycle agent behind the girls standing on the pavement that belonged to Edward Gittoes

Leonard Mckaig, Headmaster, fills his pipe after visiting Mrs Winifred Davies' Post and Telegraph Office. Lipton's tea is advertised in one window and clothing on display in the other, lit by an oil lamp. The blacksmith chats to men from John Lingen's builder's yard to the left

Set into the wall, just by the bucket to the left of the steps, was one of the taps that supplied the town with water. The house behind the children, Bank House, was where the McKaigs moved from Monument House. The large white building, Wayside, was a temperance hotel run by William Shewell, the gentleman in the foreground

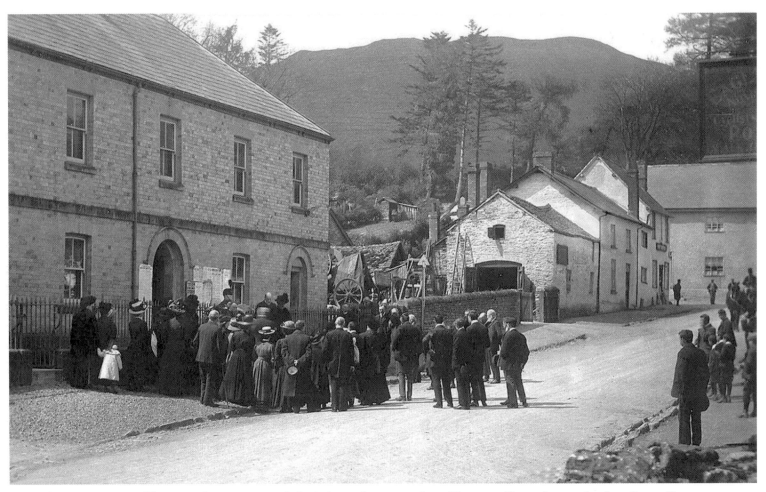

A solemn moment. The men have removed their hats. Someone in military uniform has arrived to formally announce the death of King Edward VII and the accession of his second son George V. There was no radio or television in 1910

In August 1926, The Prince of Wales visited Llandrindod Wells for a Boy Scout Jamboree. New Radnor put out flags and a floral arch over the bridge with a large fleur-de-lis, hoping to greet him, but the royal visitor drove through the town at speed. In this snap shot of the car, he can just be seen in his military uniform. Photo by A & G McKaig

The Old Parsonage, also known as The Steppes
or The Old Oak

Ted Davies stands at the entrance to The Old Swan
Inn that was opposite The Old Parsonage

This is the western entrance to New Radnor showing The Porth farm. There used to be a gate across the road and The Toll House is still there on the right

Thomas Davies and Son, millers at Haines Mill. The waterpower came from the steep sided Harley Valley about half a mile west of New Radnor. The principal crops of the area in 1914 were recorded as wheat, oats, barley and turnips

This postcard of handbell ringers made an attractive Christmas card. Bellringers today, using the same bells, continue the tradition of spreading seasonal good cheer. Left to right: Tom Price, Jack Thomas, Charlie Chubb, and Dick Thomas

Thomas Gittoes the blacksmith in New Radnor had his forge opposite Billy McKaig's workshop.
He took several photographs of him at work

The New Radnor blacksmith taken some years later

The Gittoes family outside their house in Broad Street

Shoeing Competition Prize Winners and Judges, 18 December 1908. Second from the right is Thomas Price from Penybont and the next man with two certificates is Thomas Gittoes form New Radnor

Horses being bought and sold outside The Eagle family
hotel and posting house, owned by James Niblett. On Fair
days it was traditional to eat goose served with swede and
potatoes followed by a solid rice and raisin pudding

Sheep pens outside The King's Arms during
the Sheep Fair

On 29 October every street was full of animals and men for the annual New Radnor Horse & Cattle Fair

Moving horses in Water Street during the October Fair

Vale of Radnor Agricultural Association Meeting at Walton, 1908. Everyone congregated outside The Crown Inn. There were competitions for ploughing, hedge laying and horse shoeing

Ploughing Match spectators at The Vale of Radnor Agricultural Association Meeting at Walton, 1908

Ploughing Match spectators at The Vale of Radnor Agricultural Association Meeting at Walton, 1909.
The short man with his hands on his hips is Arthur Smith, apprenticed to Thomas Gittoes, who emigrated to Australia after the First World War

28 October was the annual Sheep Fair. Sheep are seen here in pens on both sides of Broad Street as they were all through the town. Children often took a day off from school to help

Judging Sheep at a Vale of Radnor Agricultural Association Meeting

The sheep judges and spectators

Washing sheep before shearing

Harley Cottage was a small property at the entrance to Harley Valley, now in ruins

Looking west from the Castle Hill this photo shows Highgate Farm that belonged to William Phillips, opposite Haines Mill, and the steep slope of The Mynd beyond

This beautiful photo of Hereford cattle was taken behind The Vron farm, just to the west of New Radnor

Thomas Hughes of The Yatt, Old Radnor had this photo portrait of his Hereford bull taken by McKaig

A steep lane called Mutton Dingle winds up hill frtom New Radnor towards The Wimble

The Four Stones prehistoric monument stands in the centre of the Radnor valley. The wealth of ancient sites here attracted the attention of Alfred Watkins when he was looking for the straight track alignments between them called Ley-lines. At Walton half a mile east from here, the site of a 3,000-year-old woodhenge has been discovered recently

Standing by the gate to Harpton Court, halfway between Old and New Radnor, are Len and Susie, children of Jack Standen, the butler. The gatehouse is said to have been designed by the Welsh architect John Nash, 1752-1835, who was responsible for much of the layout of Regency London including Trafalgar Square and Buckingham Palace

Carriages drove up an avenue of lime trees from the entrance of Harpton Court to the residence of Sir Henry Duff Gordon. Harpton is mentioned in Domesday Book and the Lewis family was there from the fifteenth century to 1911. The main building was demolished in the mid-1950s

Harpton Court with its croquet lawn.
The estates of Downton, which stood on the north side of what is now the A44 about a mile east of New Radnor, and Harpton were the biggest employers of people in this area

Three housemaids employed at Harpton

Spring cleaning at Harpton

The Hamer girls in charge of the first washing machine at Downton. One worked the pump to draw up water, the others took turns to rock the paddle back and forth to wash the clothes with Lux soap flakes. The girl on the left is turning a small wringer that is attached to one end

Harpton Estate maintenance staff, 1910

Harpton Estate employees' Football Match, 4th February 1911, the Marrieds Team.
Left to right: Back row: (not known), Walter Watkins, Arthur Jone, Jim Niblett, William Bounds
Front row: Edward Jones,(not known), Tom Stephens, George Williams, Wilfred Haywood, Sam Bartholomew

Harpton Estate employees' Football Match, the Singles Team. 4th February 1911

The Gamekeepers. Sam Bartholomew is second from right

Vale of Radnor Hedging Competition, 1908

GWR, New Radnor Station. The railway was built in 1875. Mr John Burgess was Station Master in 1906

There were three trains a day before 1914. They were not expected to travel faster than 25mph on this branch line from Kington

Telegraph poles follow the railway track to New Radnor. Engine drivers were known to stop near here, The Bryn crossing, to set their rabbit wires and collect their trophies on the return journey

The Quarry at Dolyhir produced a large range of concrete garden furniture. The Staff at Dolyhir Railway Station have included some in their platform flower garden

The Station at Kington, Herefordshire. Large posters of seaside resorts are on display to attract holidaymakers

Billy took a series of photos of all the Railway stations from New Radnor to here at Leominster. This one was taken from the bridge, seconds later he would have being enveloped in a cloud of smoke from the approaching steam train. The white building is advertising Jos. Cooke and Sons, Pinsley Flour Mills

Train approaching Titley. Titley was the junction between the Leominster to Kington line (built 1857) and the branches, south to Lyonshall, Almeley and Eardisley (built 1874), and north to Presteign (built 1875)

The station at Presteign. The posters advertise 'K' Boots, Irvines Wines and one, GWR Summer Extras, is dated 1908)

A flying machine that landed at Colva caused quite a sensation in 1912. Sightseers from Kington, Hay, and New Radnor walked miles to see it. Mr. Corbet Wilson was racing Mr. Allen to be the first to cross the Irish Sea when he was forced down here with engine trouble. Later he crashed in the sea and was drowned

French Aero Club Balloon Race 1914. Monsieur Dollfus' balloon near The Vron, New Radnor with the owner standing at the right in a light coat. The policeman standing by the basket is Sergeant Ernest Hitchman

Cricket in the Rectory Garden. with the sons of Revd. Garnon -Williams. Left to right: Jocelyn, Neville, Kenneth, Harold, and Basil (with the larger ball). Dresses were acceptable clothing for little boys in Edwardian time

Billy must have got down on his knees for this delightful shot. White lace round her bonnet, cape and skirt—children's clothes would often reflect a mother's needleworking skills in the days when most clothes were handmade

In an era of big hats this one would have seemed quite reasonable for baby Florrie Watson

Lambs that are orphaned become very tame when reared on a bottle. The original image of this particular postcard had faded so badly that it was difficult to see what it was, but thanks to the computer this attractive scene has been restored

The wedding of Arthur Williams and Mabel Niblett, to which the McKaig family were invited. Leonard stands behind the bride with Susannah at the left of the group. Billy McKaig signed the certificate as a witness

Arthur McKaig married Mary Griffiths
on 4th October 1911

Billy's parents Leonard and Susannah McKaig retired after 24 years teaching at New Radnor School. Susannah had the youngest class and taught all the girls needlework. Leonard also played the organ at church and conducted the choir

Schoolchildren on a nature walk in 1911

School attendance fluctuated with the seasons and the harvesting of crops; one year the summer holiday started a week early because the winberries were ripe for picking. But Leonard McKaig's firm discipline gradually increased daily attendance. The school punishment book records his occasional use of a cane on the hand for bad behaviour

Mr. W.J. Gardner became the schoolmaster 1911. New desks were installed along with improved heating as a single fire in each room proved inadequate. Classroom temperatures in winter, as recorded in the school log, had often been between four and ten degrees Celsius (40-50°F) and only once reached sixteen degrees (60°F)

This peaceful village scene is by the Post Office in Evenjobb, run by Mrs. Griffiths

Brook House, Evenjobb

The blacksmith at the crossroads in Evenjobb was William Tipton.
There was also a wheelwright by the Post Office run by Thomas Evans

Every village had a blacksmith and their work with horses was often the subject of painters and photographers. Here William Tipton of Evenjobb fixes a loose shoe. The forge building today, though unused for fifty years, is very much as it was. There are two holes in the ceiling where a carthorse once reared up and punched its hooves through the plaster

Evencoyd School built 1864. In the early 1900s when this was taken,
Jethro Parkhouse was the master

Postcards of church interiors were popular with visitors. Evencoyd Church has this unusual metal screen. The hymn numbers, the white altar cloth, and the lilies indicate the photo was taken at Eastertide

St. Stephen's Church, Old Radnor, on a cloudy day. Normally there is an extensive view across the valley of Radnor to the hills. Billy took several views of the outside of the church and also the lych-gate, whilst inside he took one of the ancient font, the medieval organ case and screen, and the east window

Gladestry. This view includes the newly built rectory on the left

This postcard was sent to Sarah Pugh who worked as a maid at Cascob Rectory: 'Dear Sarah, I thought you would like a view of kinnerton church. It was a pity you was not able to come down home last Sunday I thought you would have been there by your PC best Love from Agnes'. Billy published this view even though the glass negative had obviously broken

Stapleton Castle, on the summit of a hill in the village, was founded about 1150.
The present ruins are of a sixteenth-century house on the medieval site

Lynhelyn Pool, Llanfihangel-nant-mellan. George Davies The Pool stands on the left. In 1886 the children had a half-holiday from school to watch 'the loosing' of all the water

The Forest Inn, Llanfihangel-nant-mellan, owned by Henry Price. Billy McKaig wrote one of his own postcards and sent it to Fred Davies in Llandegley about a cycle he had repaired for him: 'I will have the old cycle at the Forest Inn tomorrow night, at eight o'clock. If you are not there I will leave it. Yours W.H. McKaig'

Richard Harding L.R.C.P. Edin., surgeon, medical officer and public vaccinator, New Radnor district, lived at The Laurels, Broad Street. He was the owner of the first car in New Radnor

I like the old tablecloth and sack that gives this portrait a rural-studio look! This must have been an early attempt at portraiture using his brother Arthur as subject. He had joined the Kington and Radnorshire Bank as a clerk in 1895 at £128 per annum. Cigarettes were becoming popular

Portrait of Blanche Harding,
daughter of Dr. Richard Harding

'Season's Greeting from E.H.M.' was written across
this portrait of Elizabeth Maun picking roses in
Springfield garden. She married Walter Morgan of
Briar Lee

Florrie Watson's family (see also p.62)

The Watkins family. Back row: Bill, Arthur, Fred Powell, Joan. Middle row: Norah, Granny Amy with Geoff, Lucy, Bessie, Annie Powell née Watkins. Front row: Gwen, Kath, Minnie, Nellie, Leonard, Ronald.
Gwen could just remember McKaig and told me that he was known as Billy

Edwardian teenagers pose by a gate
—when real fur was fashionable

Mr. Parry of Smatcher Cottage

Llandegley Church Choir, 1875.

Postcard of an old photo of the Llandgley Choir of 1875. Back. row: Mary Evans, Miss Vaughan, John Duggan, Mr. Vaughan, Lisa Smythe, Jones Blacksmith. Middle row: Alice, Mr. Wheeldon, Mrs. Wheeldon, Polly Evans, Miss Wheeldon. Front row: Kittie Wilding, Anne, Blacksmith's daughter, Nell Evans. I have left a sample here of Billy's initials, WHMcK, as he signed most of his cards